How To Stop Being A Hoe

The Ultimate Guide on How to Not Be A Hoe

Patrick Smith

Table of Contents

Chapter 1

Understanding the Concept of Being A "Hoe"

If you approach another guy and ask him for his hoe, there is a 50/50 chance that you will fight. But, why is that? All you had to do was ask for his gardening tool. A hoe is a long-handled gardening tool with a thin metal blade that is frequently used at weddings, according to the dictionary. So, how did hoes become whores, and why did people turn gardening tools into slang for women who practice the oldest craft?

The word hoe originates in Old High German, the earliest stage of the German language, which lasted from approximately 500/750 to 1050 A.C. It was a variant of "houwa" that referred to a mattock or pickaxe. The word "house" was also used in 12th-century French (Old French).

In the English language, the word hoe comes from Middle English. It is a dialect of English that was spoken from the Norman (Viking) Conquest of 1066 until the late fifteenth century. Some etymologists believe Vikings introduced the term to Europe. Between 1325 and 1375, the word "hoe" became part of English. The Middle English word howe is derived from the Old French house and the German haue. From the 14th century to the 1960s, it was simply a gardening tool with a flat blade. And then something changed.

Hoe has been pronounced a whore by black men since around 1960. The term hoe is closely linked to hip-hop and rap music. However, gardening tools played no role in inspiring this type of etymology outcome. Hoes did not turn into whores. It was the opposite way around.

It just so happens that removing the r from whore results in "whoe," which is pronounced as hoe, which is probably why it's spelled that way. Why remove the letter r? Because it was African-American English. In most cases, African Americans omitted the final r from their pronunciations. As a result, the gardening tool known as a hoe simply had an unlucky match.

What comes to mind when you hear the word "hoe? Most of us are conditioned to believe it is a word for women who sleep a lot. When you look at Urban Dictionary, the definitions can be unsettling and often sexist. But, in our defense, it is what we have been conditioned to believe. The term "hoe" appears to be used only to describe women in popular culture and the media. The word "hoe" is used so frequently in pop music and rap, and 99 percent of the references are to women.

I feel like there is so much pressure to have a hoe phase when you are young or newly single. People frequently asked me if I was going to go through a hoe phase after I broke up with my two-year boyfriend. I didn't think of that right away. But, feeling peer pressure and messages from the media that hoeing is a natural thing in your 20s, I attempted to participate in one. The "hoe phase" lasted approximately four months. During that time, I had one one-night stand, slept with someone twice after a second date, and then slept with the same person for seven months straight. Was this even considered the hoe phase? I never slept with more than one person at a time, so does that count? I thought I was supposed to feel liberated during this phase, but I was more upset because the men I had slept with either ghosted me or lied about things.

I believe we fail to communicate to people that it is acceptable not to participate in a hoe phase. There is nothing wrong with participating in one, but it is also acceptable to opt-out. It is perfectly acceptable to be celibate simply because you are young and newly single! Neither is better than the other. However, it is critical to listen to yourself and avoid engaging in activities motivated by peer pressure or media images.

I felt slightly gross as I started the hoe phase and told my friends. I'm not sure if it was because I had so many negative associations with the word, or if I had imposter syndrome. I found it strange that others might have thought of me as a hoe, putting me in the same negative category as those in rap and television. I did not consider myself superior to these women, but the negative connotation bothered me.

So, what's the solution? At first, I thought we should just accept calling men hoes. As a result, the word would become gender-neutral, and men would no longer be able to associate it with negativity. So I started referring to men as hoes who slept with a lot of women because that's what they did to us. I began to refer to rappers and regular men who boasted about sleeping with women as hoes. But the problem is that men never seemed to take offense to this, so it never caught on. Men also believe they are magical and enjoy using the "lock vs. key" analogy. To them, they are the key, and a key that can unlock all the locks is a valuable master key. But women are the lock, and if every key can unlock this one lock, the lock is worthless. How do you bring logic into this mindset? The only other option, in my opinion, is to refrain from automatically associating the term "hoe" with negative things when it refers solely to women.

People who choose sexual liberation are not hoes. Also, perhaps we should all stop worrying about other people's sex lives. If it does not involve or harm us, we should not have the right to characterize women as hoes.

Chapter 2

Understanding The Implications Of Promiscuity And How It Affects Personal Well-Being

Casual sex attitudes tend to evolve as people's lives and relationship statuses change. Depending on the situation, it is celebrated, savored, criticized, envied, or stigmatized. Some people take it seriously, weighing all of the potential mental and physical consequences, rewards, and drawbacks before engaging in casual sex.

Whether you prefer to go with the flow or dispute the details, consider the cultural background and potential mental health consequences of casual sex before choosing if it's suitable for you.

Casual sex means something different to each person. In general, the word refers to consensual sex that occurs outside of a romantic relationship or marriage, with no strings attached or any expectation of commitment or exclusivity.

It may occur between lovers only once or on a regular basis, planned or spontaneously. It might be a work colleague, close friend, former romantic partner, casual acquaintance, or total stranger.

A casual sex encounter or arrangement may also be referred to as a hookup, one-night stand, tryst, booty call, friends-with-benefits relationship, or a variety of other euphemisms.

Casual sex is essentially a way to enjoy sexual intimacy without the emotional, practical, or romantic elements of love or a committed relationship. Some people engage in occasional casual sex interactions. Others do it more frequently, and they may have one or more partners with whom they interact on a regular basis.

Casual sex does not always involve intercourse. It could involve any number of actions that are considered physically intimate, such as reciprocal masturbation, kissing, oral sex, and penetration.

Some people regard casual sex as a healthy sexual outlet, similar to regular exercise, or a satisfying physical experience. Some people like casual sex because it eliminates the expectations, accountability, and pressures of a typical love relationship.

Others find casual sex appealing, but controlling emotions becomes challenging, resulting in damaged sentiments or unrequited longing. Others believe the hazards, such as sexually transmitted infections, sexual misconduct, and disappointment, are too high and/or that sex should only occur in a committed or married relationship.

Casual sex is frequently presented in films as carefree romps that result in a bright, enthusiastic glow and, on occasion, romance. Other representations result in disappointment, remorse, and heartache.

Some believe that sex outside of commitment is sinful or exclusively appropriate for men or "loose" women. These encounters can often be considered infidelity if one or both of the individuals are in another relationship. Clearly, prejudices, assumptions, ethics, experience, and personal convictions all come into play. Furthermore, a few terrible or good casual sex encounters might significantly alter a person's attitude toward the practice.

We can all agree that casual (or any) intercourse increases the risk of unexpected pregnancy, sexually transmitted diseases (STIs), and physical/emotional harm from your partner, especially if you do not know them well. However, in addition to moral concerns and danger problems, there are mental health consequences to consider when determining whether casual sex is emotionally good for you.

Potential Drawbacks and Benefits

Casual sex has advantages and disadvantages that vary depending on the circumstances and people involved. Each individual should consider any underlying shame or other bad feelings that they may experience or be exposed to. It's also vital to consider how likely you are to feel positive about the event before, during, and after.

Potential Drawbacks

Potential downsides, such as emotional distress and sexual regret, vary greatly from person to person, primarily depending on thinking, past, and expectations. As previously stated, participating in casual intercourse has significant bodily dangers, including STIs, unwanted pregnancy, and sexual assault. This is especially true if safe sexual practices are not followed. However, the emotional consequences can be just as severe, especially if casual sex is used to escape or bury feelings.

Anecdotally, many people join these interactions hoping to have fun, only to become attached, disappointed, irritated, or confused.

Possible Benefits

On the other hand, many others are pleasantly pleased by their experiences and capacity to appreciate a basic physical interaction. Other often mentioned advantages include physical intimacy, meeting a prospective life partner, attractiveness, and sexual fulfillment.

Mental Health Effects

Some people are better at distinguishing between romantic and sexual urges. Others readily associate emotions and touch, making casual sex more difficult to maintain, regardless of intentions. According to research, women have a more difficult time preventing emotional attachment than males, and when this occurs, they are more likely to feel used, depressed, regretful, or ashamed later on.

Some people rush in without considering how they would feel afterward, only to be left with hurt, guilt, or emptiness. Despite convincing yourself that it's simply sex for enjoyment, you may feel more. So it's critical to examine expectations honestly.

Other people have the opposite problem: they are so focused on keeping the relationship exclusively physical that they overlook the possibility of a long-term, deep relationship and are later upset that they did not seek one when they had the opportunity. Still, others enjoy the pure physical thrills of a booty call.

Casual sex relationships can have a skewed power dynamic, with one party wanting more, such as frequency or type of commitment, while the other prefers to keep things casual. This is likely to lower the former's self-esteem, resulting in anxiety, panic, self-doubt, and even melancholy.

Furthermore, research reveals that post-hookup sadness and concerns are more probable with unprotected sex, as well as if an encounter goes on longer than planned or if either party felt compelled to undertake sexual actions they did not want to do.

Acting against conservative views about casual sex is exhilarating for some, but disappointing or even devastating for others.

The evidence on the mental health impacts of casual sex is divided. Some studies have identified a link between casual sex and a number of negative mental health outcomes, including anxiety, melancholy, feeling awful about oneself, regret, despair, and low self-esteem. However, many others have reported beneficial effects such as increased self-esteem, relaxation, sexual satisfaction, and self-awareness.

In fact, a comprehensive 2020 evaluation of 71 studies indicated that most persons experienced favorable emotional outcomes as a result of casual sex. However, the researchers point out that positive mental health effects are not universal, and that factors like drinking alcohol, not knowing one's partner, and not being sexually happy with the meeting can all increase the likelihood of a negative emotional response.

Surprisingly, numerous studies have indicated that women who engage in more frequent hookups have a larger positive link with negative emotional consequences, whereas men have the reverse effect: more casual sex produces more pleasant sensations.

Finally, your personal experiences and beliefs about sexuality, gender roles, sense of self, romance, religion, morality, life purpose, and happiness will influence how you see and consider casual sex. Essentially, it is different for everyone, and only you can determine what is best for you.

According to research, the behavior is widespread and becoming more socially acceptable. Many teenagers and young adults prefer casual hookups as starting points to romantic relationships over traditional dating methods, viewing sex as both a physical need and a means of screening potential romantic partners.

Casual sex is highly common among teenagers and young adults, as well as people who are not in committed partnerships. In one study, 40% of those in their early twenties reported a recent casual sex encounter. Other studies revealed that more than half of 18- to 24-year-olds engaged in the activity. Among sexually active teenagers, nearly 40% reported encounters rather than exclusive relationships.

Other surveys estimate that more than 70% of young adults engage in casual sex. The number of previous sexual partners, amount of finished education, alcohol and drug usage, and attitude all influenced the number of casual sex experiences. For example, people pursuing college degrees were less likely to engage in casual intercourse than those who did not complete high school.

Dating applications like Tinder, Grindr, OkCupid, Bumble and Coffee Meets Bagel have provided users with a variety of dating and casual sex alternatives, in addition to lowering the stigma associated with non-committal sex.

Another review discovered that religious belief, strong self-esteem, and having married parents reduced the risk of the behavior, but race, socioeconomic position, depression, and being in a romantic relationship had no effect on casual sex rates.

Casual sex can be perceived as a gift, required pleasure, joyous indulgence, slight regret, or severe humiliation, depending on the individual. The decision to engage in casual sex is a personal one that is shaped by a variety of factors, including your relationship status, life experiences, and attitudes toward casual sex and possible partners.

Finally, the crucial thing to remember is that there is no right or wrong answer, only what feels best to you. It can be beneficial to grasp the difference or overlap between sex and love for yourself, as well as if you want to keep them separate.

You may discover how you feel about hookups by trial and error, but even better: Consider what you want and believe about your sexuality and sexual behaviors to truly understand what is ideal for you.

If thinking about casual sex makes you feel more excited and empowered than ashamed or guilty, it's a good sign. Obtaining proper consent and following safe sex procedures are also required.

The form of casual sex you are considering may have an impact on your satisfaction and comfort level. For example, anonymous sex may feel heated, lonely, or unclean in a negative way. Hooking up with an ex or close friend may feel comfortable, safe, boring, or naughty in a positive manner. Consent is also an important consideration. To have a great experience with casual sex, make sure you're doing what you want to do and aren't feeling compelled (or forced) to do anything you don't want to.

Alternatively, sleeping with a platonic friend may be difficult, especially if one of you develops romantic sentiments that the other does not reciprocate, and having sex with a former flame may open a can of worms you'd prefer to keep closed. Also, if casual sex feels incompatible with your moral views, you may have difficulty enjoying it; yet, you may realize that your attitudes about uncommitted sex change as you grow as a person and a sexual being.

The trick is to honestly analyze how you feel about the concept of casual sex and what you actually want to gain from the encounter. Casual sex may be appropriate for those who wish to explore a variety of sexual behaviors and relationships before committing to a monogamous relationship. You may want to discover your own sexuality and wants, and you may feel more at ease doing so in a casual situation. If you simply enjoy hookups (or want to), go ahead and have some.

Some people's sexuality is more closely linked to intimate connections than others, who are more at ease divorcing their sexual wants and desires from being in love and/or in a relationship, and either approach can be healthy and something to appreciate.

Casual sex can either be fantastic or leave you feeling guilty, empty, or unfulfilled. You'll know it's emotionally healthy for you if it makes you feel good and confident in yourself. If not, you may not be in the correct state of mind to enjoy the experience. Understand that everyone is in a different place, which will most likely change over time, and that's okay.

While some people leave a carnal experience feeling unhappy, embarrassed, or sad, others may feel more confident, at peace, fulfilled, or pleased. If you fall into the latter category, you may wish to work through feelings of shame or longing, or you may choose to limit your sexual activity to romantic relationships.

In the end, decide for yourself whether or not casual sex is appropriate for your sexual journey, values, and ambitions.

Chapter 3

Unpacking Cultural and Social Influences

In a study, researchers discovered that characteristics like this one that influence a young person's sexual practices are startlingly similar around the world. Because people aged 15 to 24 account for roughly half of all new HIV infections worldwide, modifying sexual behavior in this age range is critical to combating disease spread, according to the researchers. They believe their findings can help design more successful safe-sex initiatives.

The findings also explain why so many HIV programs have been ineffective. These initiatives primarily focus on non-social causes for young people's lack of condom use, such as ignorance and access difficulties. As a result, organizations that solely provide information and condoms while ignoring the critical social elements described are only addressing a portion of the problem.

Researchers from the Medical Research Council in the United Kingdom analyzed 268 papers on sexual conduct in young people aged 10 to 25 published between 1990 and 2004. The review incorporated data from several countries, including the United Kingdom, Australia, Mexico, and South Africa.

They identified seven similar themes by using computer techniques to sort through the research; five of these had to do with sexual activity in general and two with the usage of condoms in particular. The findings highlight potential reasons why a teen or young adult would position themselves in a risky sexual scenario.

When it comes to condom use, both men and women rely on perception to determine whether or not they require condom protection. In one research, a male from the United Kingdom said, "It depends on how 'easy' a woman is. If she slept with me the first night, I'd use a condom. However, if I met a female who was not that type of girl and began seeing her on a regular basis, I would trust her. "I don't like wearing them."

All of the societies investigated had strikingly comparable expectations for sexual behavior in both genders, with men expected to be highly heterosexually active and women chaste. For example, it is acceptable for men to seek sexual fulfillment, but a woman on the prowl can be labeled as "loose" or "cheap."

When a guy makes a sexual approach, many women might hesitate to say "yes" right away out of fear of being labeled as awkward. According to the experts, this complicates the interpretation of "no". In one of the studies studied, a young male stated, "When women say 'no,' they mean 'yes.'" A lady can never say 'let's do it' clearly. You should read her facial expression. If she continues to repeat "no" and closes her eyes, then she wants it.

For guys, there is sometimes a shame associated with a lack of experience or failing to score with a female. Young males who do not have sex with their girlfriends may face accusations of being 'gay.' According to the scientists' research article, some people are concerned that they may be unable to penetrate the condom and may even avoid using it for fear of losing their erection.

Since the introduction of HIV and AIDS, there has been an increase in sexual behavior research, with the majority of studies focusing on detecting and modifying sexual habits. Inquiries like "What proportion of young individuals claimed to have used protection the first time they had sex?" were part of this quantitative study.

While this knowledge can be valuable, the scientists stated that it is less relevant for understanding the causes of sexual behavior. Qualitative research aids in the description and explanation of behavior as well as its social context.

The findings could explain, for example, why a woman would avoid using condoms while having high levels of understanding and access to protection because she believes her partner is "clean," or she does not want to look too experienced with sexual interactions. Using these seven categories, policymakers might create a local profile of factors influencing sexual habits. This might be used as a template to brief public health practitioners and determine which safe-sex campaigns are most likely to succeed.

One option for future research into sexual behavior is to focus on deviants, or those who do not adhere to these seven norms. The study might look at which guys deny intercourse and why, as well as what distinguishes young individuals who insist on condoms even when they are in long-term relationships.

Defying Preconceptions And Celebrating Originality In Sexual Expression

In recent years, discussions around gender and sexuality have gained traction, challenging established standards and building a more inclusive society. Breaking out from the binary view of gender and acknowledging the fluidity of sexuality has paved the way for understanding and acceptance.

Gender is a social construct that includes a variety of identities other than the binary categories of male and female. It is critical to acknowledge that gender is not exclusively established by biological sex, but rather by a very personal and unique experience. Some people identify as the gender they were assigned at birth (cisgender), while others identify as transgender, non-binary, genderqueer, or gender-neutral. Each identity represents a distinct expression and understanding of gender.

Recognizing the diversity of gender identities allows us to question cultural expectations and preconceptions that limit people's ability to express themselves. Everyone deserves the freedom to discover and appreciate their true selves, regardless of cultural conventions or expectations.

17

Sexuality refers to a person's emotional, romantic, and sexual desires. It covers a wide range of sexual orientations, including bisexuality, heterosexuality, homosexuality, asexuality, and many more. Sexual orientation is an inherent part of one's identity that should be acknowledged without judgment or discrimination.

It is critical to recognize that sexual orientation is not a choice, but rather an intrinsic trait. By accepting and embracing different sexual orientations, we foster an inclusive environment in which everyone can live authentically and without fear of prejudice or shame.

Education and awareness are essential for creating a more welcoming society. By learning about various gender identities and sexual orientations, we may dispel myths and fight deeply rooted cultural biases.

Creating safe venues for people to express their gender and sexuality is critical. This includes giving access to information, support groups, and mental health treatments tailored to the specific requirements of different communities. Furthermore, it is critical to support inclusive policies at all levels, including educational facilities, companies, and government agencies.

By embracing diversity and challenging established conventions, we can build a world in which everyone feels seen, heard, and appreciated. It is critical to remember that gender and sexual orientation do not define a person's worth; they are simply parts of their identity. Celebrating variety enhances our communities and enables us to learn from each other's unique experiences.

Chapter 4

Cultivating Self-Worth And Respect

Self-esteem is mentioned in the literature as a factor that influences the practice of risky sexual behaviors. It is commonly considered that higher levels of self-esteem are linked to safer sexual practices, particularly those that prevent HIV transmission. The study literature was evaluated to investigate the link between self-esteem and the use of safer sexual behaviors. According to research, adolescents who engage in riskier sexual behaviors and have a larger number of sexual partners have greater levels of self-esteem.

Self-esteem influences all aspects of your life, including relationships, friendships, your work life, and, yes, your sexual encounters. Low self-esteem can take away the enjoyment of most activities, including sex. That's because sexuality is a complex interplay of emotional, cultural, physiological, psychological, and interpersonal elements, all of which are linked to self-esteem.

Self-esteem is an individual's assessment of themselves, determining if they are capable, loveable, and deserving of happiness. To really enjoy your sexuality, you must have a strong self-esteem. Without self-esteem, you may doubt your partner's love and affection since you do not feel deserving of it. In fact, the intersection of self-esteem and sexuality has given rise to the term "sexual self-esteem."

Self-esteem is an individual's assessment of themselves, determining if they are capable, loveable, and deserving of happiness.

Sexual self-esteem is a word that describes how you perceive your sexual identity. It has several components, including whether you think you're sexually attractive or capable. How you perceive yourself in sexual situations is a critical component of sexual self-esteem. Your opinion of your sexual potential is also related to your body image, or how you perceive your body. People who consider they are unattractive are more prone to have low self-esteem.

Low sexual self-esteem can be caused by a variety of circumstances, including a history of emotional, physical, or sexual abuse, emotional or sexual humiliation, or being called pejorative names. If your age, skin tone, weight, or other physical attributes make you feel unattractive, you may also suffer from low sexual self-esteem. Even those who adhere to society's definition of "beautiful" may suffer from sexual self-esteem issues as a result of internal worries or external pressures.

Researchers have gone so far as to declare low sexual self-esteem a "disability. This is because people with poor sexual self-esteem are more prone to participate in riskier sexual behaviors, such as unprotected sex and putting themselves in dangerous/damaging circumstances. Because of internal concerns or beliefs, people with poor sexual self-esteem are less likely to trust healthy sexual interactions. As such, your sexuality is inextricably linked to your self-esteem, and vice versa.

How Self-Esteem Affect Your Sexuality

Sexual motivations
Most people know that making bad sexual decisions is a direct result of having low self-esteem, whereas making good sexual decisions is a result of having high self-esteem. If you have high self-esteem, you are more likely to make decisions based on your desires, and you will feel comfortable enforcing those decisions. For example, if you are sexually attracted to someone but do not want to engage in safe sex, you will feel confident enough to walk away rather than give in to the ultimatum.

A lack of self-esteem can lead to the mistaken belief that your sexuality is all you have to offer. This internal notion can motivate you to have sex with someone you don't want to have sex with or to remain in settings where you are not respected. Meanwhile, healthy self-esteem empowers you to pursue sexual partners based on genuine desires, which boosts your self-esteem even more.

Self-Confidence
Self-esteem, confidence, and sexuality are inextricably related. A healthy sex life makes you more confident, which boosts your self-esteem. Possessing a strong sense of self-worth encourages you to explore your sexuality and enjoy your relationships in a healthy way, which makes you seem more certain and, thus, more attractive.

But the opposite is also true. Low self-esteem can also contribute to a loss of sexual confidence. This can emerge in a variety of ways, including arrogant sexual attempts and overstated assertions. This demonstrates that self-esteem is critical for confidence and sex appeal.

Body image
Most of us are self-conscious about some aspects of our bodies. While some self-examination is natural and necessary, an unhealthy fixation with your body and looks can lead to unwanted sexual experiences. If you have severe body image issues, you are more likely to focus on that body part during sex out of fear that your partner will judge you based on it.

This could make you plan ways to hide that body area or make excuses for it all the time, which would ruin your whole sex experience. Furthermore, partners frequently interpret your obsession with your body as a lack of interest in them, which can exacerbate your sexual experience. Meanwhile, people with high self-esteem can devote their entire lives to the pursuit of pleasure.

Developing Positive Sexual Self-Esteem
If you believe you have low sexual self-esteem or recognize yourself in the examples above, there are several steps you can take to address the issue. If you're unhappy with your body, you can

investigate the causes of your dissatisfaction and remind yourself not to pursue unhealthy and arbitrary beauty goals.

If your low self-esteem is resulting in relationship problems, it is beneficial to have an open discussion with your partner. This will provide them with the necessary information and tools to collaborate with and assist you. If you believe you have extremely low self-esteem, it may be beneficial to seek professional advice and pursue therapy.

So, to boost your sexual self-esteem, here are some strategies for increasing positive thoughts, feelings, and behaviors:

I am a good lover, which is a positive thought.
Whether you are a good kisser, masseuse, gentle touch, or fabulous licker, whatever defines your specialty contributes to your identity as a lover. Celebrate what you know and proceed from there.

I believe that being a sexual god or goddess is a great sensation
I know it's a cliché, but self-affirming comments like "I am good enough and people like me" actually work. To develop healthy and strong sexual self-esteem, you must first recognize that you are not inferior to anyone else. Feeling like a sexual god/goddess can make you feel seductive, intriguing, and alluring. Who doesn't enjoy that?

I'm going to live in the now
It is a positive behavior to demonstrate. Living in the present moment is essential for developing strong sexual self-esteem. Instead of dwelling on the past or attempting to foresee the future, simply live in the present moment.

I feel good, which is a wonderful feeling
While it may not seem significant in developing positive sexual self-esteem, it is. Feeling good before or during a sexual experience helps you relax and become more aware of your body's reactions and responses.

My body is my temple, and I am in control of this experience.
It is a positive concept and likely one of the most vital beliefs to hold. Whatever your sexual pleasure, you should be in control of the encounter. This does not imply that you must be in charge of initiating sex or sexual actions, but rather that you have control over what is and is not permitted to occur based on your degree of comfort.

Understand that this is not an exhaustive list of positive thoughts, attitudes, or behaviors to cultivate. This is a suggestion or a starting point for you to create your own list as you develop your sexual self-esteem. However, just remembering that you deserve fantastic sex, feeling good about yourself, and repeating the experience might help you feel more confident in your sexuality.

Creating Boundaries And Learning To Prioritize Personal Beliefs And Integrity.

Defining your personal beliefs can be a guidance when making decisions about your profession or scheduling more time for self-care. But what exactly does it mean to have personal values, and how do you determine your own?

You might not keep a list of values in your desk drawer. However, the decisions you've made throughout your life are likely to reflect a pattern of priorities.

Assume you place a higher priority on hitting professional milestones than on achieving your fitness goals. A new career opportunity comes your way. The recruiter says that the timetable is tough, and the job responsibilities need a steep learning curve.

However, it will motivate you to advance your profession in transforming ways. If your career ambitions are very important to you, you will most likely say "yes," even if it means skipping your 5K run training.

There are no correct or incorrect answers when it comes to your personal principles. Your genuine values cannot and should not be suppressed. They add meaning to your life and increase your self-awareness.

Without a clear grasp of them, you may struggle with self-discovery, which is the process of discovering your true self. As a result, you may struggle to make decisions, improve your profession, or have a fulfilling life.

Personal values are a set of guiding ideas and beliefs that help you distinguish between "good" and "bad." These include ideas like integrity vs dishonesty, or hard labor versus cutting corners. Everyone prioritizes their basic values differently, and yours influences how you navigate through the world.

Personal values shape your behavior, relationships, and daily life. They help you make key decisions, affect personal development, and chart your ideal job path.

Every individual has a unique set of values. What is important to you may differ from what your friends and coworkers value. However, you are more inclined to share personal core values with those closest to you. According to research, you may be more attracted to those who share your values. Partners, colleagues, and family members who share your values are strong indicators of long-term relationships.

Everyone communicates these values differently. Assume that you and your coworker both value community. Maybe you practice charity by organizing a company-wide food drive, while your coworker prepares leadership training for the entire team. These are two valid expressions for the same value.

You may be unaware of your values, but understanding them can help you advance your job, create interpersonal relationships, and use your free time more meaningfully. Understanding what matters to you might help you match your actions with your inner self.

This knowledge also assists you in reducing the harmful relationships, employment, or situations that sap your vitality, allowing you to live your happiest life. It may even make you feel more fulfilled, as engaging in activities that correspond with your values can reduce depression and anxiety and enhance your mental health.

Furthermore, having a career that reflects your values can inspire you to be more enthusiastic and meaningful at work. This will eventually help you thrive in your career since you will be more motivated to achieve well.

Personal Values versus Basic Convictions

Both personal values and core beliefs influence your decisions and behavior, but personal values are normally beneficial, whereas core beliefs are formed throughout childhood and can be destructive or false.

You may respect honesty and hard work, but you also believe that you should not express your feelings because your parents did not.

The value is something you consider essential and desire to communicate via your behavior, whereas the fundamental conviction is something you believe to be true about the world or yourself, irrespective of the evidence.

There are three kinds of core beliefs:

- ❖ *Personal beliefs*
- ❖ *Beliefs about others*
- ❖ *Global beliefs*

Adjusting these is generally more challenging than re-evaluating your values, but you can do so by clarifying your essential beliefs, noting where they came from, and reframing your perspective on the situation.

Your values are a significant element of your personal identity. They form you into your real self and provide you with a feeling of purpose and meaning, which influences your personality, goal setting, and life direction.

Your values also help you better grasp who you are. They encourage you to strive toward your goals rather than against them. You feel most like yourself when you make choices that align with your personal values.

Personal values also influence your interactions. When you understand how to express your beliefs, you can create clear boundaries, form healthy alliances, and cultivate relationships that respect your self-esteem.

Connecting with your beliefs can also help you connect with like-minded friends and coworkers. A social network that shares your beliefs can help you build more meaningful, supportive, and real relationships.

Ultimately, putting your principles first will make it easier for you to express your demands to coworkers, family, and friends. Sharing these vital feelings can improve your general well-being, whilst suppressing your emotions might have negative health consequences. Psychologists feel that connecting to essential personal values can be a powerful motivator for recovering mental health.

Self-awareness is the understanding of who you are and how you vary or align with others. Self-knowledge, or how well you understand your values, attitudes, and behaviors, is essential for growing self-awareness.

Deepening your self-awareness necessitates serious introspection. It's hard work that can force you to address behaviors, decisions, or actions that don't reflect the person you want to be. But it's a necessary first step toward self-improvement.

Although it is difficult, the self-awareness you acquire from connecting with your personal values can motivate you to be true to yourself, allowing you to make better decisions, invest in your personal growth, and create healthy connections. Furthermore, doing the necessary internal work might help you gain confidence, creativity, and emotional control.

How Personal Values Influence Your Work Life

Your personal ideals don't just apply to your personal life. Let's say one of your core principles is loyalty. This could have an impact on your dependability at work, making you a trustworthy employee.

Being a devoted employee will help you advance in your career. Your coworkers may look to you for leadership advice, and your manager may recommend you for advancement.

Alternatively, you could value honesty above all else. This may lead you to be a team player who values constructive criticism, teamwork, and integrity. That's a trait your coworkers will recognize and respect because it benefits the team.

Think about this: How does valuing self-assurance, tenacity, and perseverance affect your career? Your own values affect who you are, and thus the type of employee or leader you are.

Advantages of personal values

Personal values affect all aspects of your existence. Aside from boosting your self-awareness and relationships, here are eight ways that prioritizing your values can improve your daily life:

- ❖ *Boosts your confidence.*
- ❖ *Gives you a vision that guides your long-term ambitions.*
- ❖ *Develops a stronger feeling of purpose in your work objectives and aims*
- ❖ *Helps you handle stress by concentrating on what matters in life.*

- ❖ *Guides your decision-making with ethics, self-esteem, and integrity.*
- ❖ *Describes a leadership style based on treating others as you would like to be treated.*
- ❖ *Encourages you to be resilient during times of conflict or significant obstacles.*
- ❖ *Increases your satisfaction with choices that are consistent with your moral convictions.*

Examples of Personal Values

You may not yet know what values are essential to you. That is okay. Understanding the meaning of personal values and determining the ones you have can take time.

You might make a comprehensive list of values or just a few ideas and rate them based on their importance. The most essential thing is to live by your personal values, regardless of how you define them.

Here are some personal values examples you can use to make your list:

- ❖ *Family*
- ❖ *Courage*
- ❖ *Creativity*
- ❖ *Professional Achievements*
- ❖ *Kindness*
- ❖ *Independence*
- ❖ *Health*
- ❖ *Honesty*
- ❖ *Loyalty*
- ❖ *Determination*

How to Find Your Personal Values

You might choose your values consciously or unintentionally based on your background or culture. However, even if you understand how personal values develop, identifying the values that guide your life will most certainly require some effort.

Here are some tips to help you determine your values:

- ❖ *Going on a journey of self-discovery might help you better understand yourself.*
- ❖ *Define your short and long-term goals and the major priorities that connect them.*
- ❖ *Limit the influences of friends, family, workplace, and commitments, that attempt to define your personal values.*
- ❖ *Reflect on periods when you were most at peace and your well-being was at its peak.*
- ❖ *Consider life instances in which you thought something was missing, such as teamwork, independence, or honesty.*
- ❖ *Create a personal vision statement for your future and determine any essential principles.*

The significance of adjusting your values

Life is not static, nor are your values. Life might present you with new challenges at any time. A career, a growing family, or the end of a destructive relationship all provide opportunities for self-reflection. And as you adapt to the changes, your values evolve and alter alongside them.

Your values' relative importance may also shift. Perhaps you used to believe that work-life balance was an optional career bonus. After having a child, it may become an unavoidable priority. It is critical to adjust your values and develop goals that fit your present situation. Otherwise, a demanding career that does not allow you to prioritize your family values may leave you feeling burned out, bitter, or unmotivated.

Making it a practice to check in and re-evaluate your personal values is a terrific method to ensure that you strive for personal improvement, respect your needs, and are not influenced by limiting ideas.

Values exist in various shapes, sizes, and degrees of importance. Finding your values requires constant effort. They are not always as simple as you believe. However, they are always with you, guiding your choices and affecting your behaviors.

You may start identifying your own and live a more fulfilling life now that you know what personal values are.

Committing to figuring out what you value in life will always pay off. You will have a stronger sense of purpose, a better awareness of yourself, and the ability to make decisions that help you reach your goals in life.

Chapter 5

Managing Relationships Mindfully

Making meaningful connections with others is an important part of our own growth and development. Relationships help us better understand ourselves by learning from the experiences of others, and they foster understanding and compassion. Our relationships allow us to gain a greater understanding of ourselves and others. The relationships we form, whether with family, friends, coworkers, or even strangers, are critical to our journey of self-discovery.

From several perspectives, it is clear that our connections have a huge impact on our lives. Here are some ideas regarding how partnerships affect personal growth:

Relationships assist us develop self-awareness
Interacting with others helps us discover more about ourselves, our values, and our views. We get to see how others see us and our behaviors, which might help us identify our own strengths and faults. For example, a person may find that they have a propensity to interrupt others during conversations, something they were previously unaware of.

Relationships help us develop empathy and compassion
When we interact with others, we have a better understanding of their experiences and feelings. This understanding allows us to develop empathy and compassion for others, both of which are vital for personal growth. Connecting with someone who has experienced marginalization or discrimination, for example, may help a person obtain a greater understanding of how it feels.

Relationships offer support and encouragement
We all need encouragement and assistance as we face life's obstacles. A supporting network of people who believe in us can make a big difference in our personal development journey. For

example, a person may be more driven to pursue their aspirations if they have friends who encourage and support them.

Relationships allow us to learn new things
Connecting with people from other backgrounds and experiences allows us to learn new things and broaden our perspectives. Connecting with someone from another country, for example, may allow a person to learn about a new culture or way of living.

Building meaningful connections with people is an important part of personal development. Relationships assist us to develop self-awareness, empathy, and compassion, as well as give support encouragement, and the opportunity to master new skills. Our relationships allow us to genuinely understand ourselves and others, ultimately leading to the best version of ourselves.

Intuition

Intuition is also important in personal development and relationships. The inner voice guides us to make decisions that are consistent with our genuine selves. Intuition is a gut sense that tells us whether we should trust or avoid a person or situation. It is an innate sense that is frequently difficult to articulate but always correct. We can lead more satisfying lives if we can learn to believe in our gut.

Trusting Your Intuition in Relationships
In relationships, intuition can help us make better choices about who we invite into our lives. It can help us spot red flags early on, such as a spouse who is untrustworthy or incompatible with our values. Trusting our intuition allows us to avoid unhealthy relationships that drain our energy and leave us feeling disappointed.

Intuition and Personal Development
Intuition can also help us develop as people. It can direct us to opportunities that are in line with our passions and goals. Making choices that support personal development and fulfillment is made

possible by paying attention to our intuition, which makes us more conscious of our true goals and values.

Developing intuition

Developing intuition needs work and patience. We can begin by listening to our inner voice and writing about our intuition and emotions. Meditation and mindfulness activities can also help us connect with our intuition. It is critical to believe our intuition and not dismiss it as coincidence or unreasonable.

Balancing intuition and logic

While intuition is necessary, it must be balanced with rationality. Intuition can help us make judgments, but we must also use our rational minds to consider the pros and disadvantages. In order to make educated decisions that are authentic to ourselves, we must strike a balance between intuition and reasoning.

Benefits of Trusting Your Intuition

Living a more satisfying life can be achieved by following our instincts. It can help us avoid harmful relationships, make healthier decisions, and experience personal growth. When we trust our intuition, we gain confidence in ourselves and our skills. We learn to trust the trip and accept the unknown with open arms.

Relationships and personal development rely heavily on intuition. The inner voice guides us to make decisions that are consistent with our genuine selves. Trusting our intuition allows us to avoid harmful relationships, make better decisions, and experience personal growth. Developing intuition involves experience and patience, and it must be balanced with rationality in order to make sound decisions. Trusting our intuition can lead to a more fulfilling existence in which we learn to trust the process and welcome the uncertainty.

Chapter 6

Embracing Sexual Empowerment

The problem of female sexuality and the enjoyment gap highlights the complexities of sexual emancipation. According to research, a considerable number of women do not consistently achieve orgasm during intercourse, reflecting not only individual experiences but also greater cultural faults. The causes for this disparity are diverse, with roots in historical, cultural, and societal contexts that frequently prioritize male pleasure while ignoring women's specific sexual needs and desires.

Addressing these issues involves a multifaceted approach that includes shifts in societal attitudes, enhanced sexual education, inclusive research, and places in which women feel encouraged to explore their sexuality freely and openly. Central to this effort is the concept of permission, which is a basic, non-negotiable feature of each sexual experience that assures all partners are willing and fully involved.

However, violations of consent are quite widespread, with serious implications for individuals and society. To build a culture of respect and safety, we must address this issue through education, advocacy, and open discourse.

My experiences in both my personal and professional life have brought to light the necessity of a sex-positive strategy for both cultural change and individual empowerment. Studies have demonstrated that embracing sex positivity can improve mental health outcomes, emphasizing the relationship between sexual fulfillment, self-esteem, and overall well-being.

Sexual empowerment begins with information and progresses via open discourse, safe discussion spaces, and respect for individual needs and desires. It's a path of self-discovery in which we embrace our sexuality with joy and confidence, without guilt or shame.

In today's environment, it is critical to acknowledge the significance of accepting women's sexuality as an essential component of their identity and overall well-being.

Understanding women's sexuality

Women's sexuality is a complex component of their identity that includes desires, dreams, and relationships. It is critical to acknowledge that every woman experiences her sexuality differently, and there is no "correct" or "wrong" method of expressing or exploring it. Understanding and appreciating the diversity of women's sexuality allows us to build a more inclusive and supportive atmosphere.

Challenging Social Expectations

Throughout history, women have frequently faced cultural expectations and standards around their sexuality. It is critical to question these assumptions and foster open discussions about women's aspirations and experiences. By doing so, we can foster a society in which women feel free to express their sexuality without fear of being judged or ashamed.

Empowerment through Sexual Confidence

Embracing one's sexuality can boost self-esteem, self-awareness, and empowerment. When women are given the opportunity to explore and express their sexuality, they can gain a stronger sense of self and feel more in charge of their bodies and decisions. This empowerment can go beyond the bedroom and affect other aspects of their lives as well.

Body Positivity and Sexual Expression

Promoting body positivity is an important step towards accepting women's sexuality. By encouraging women to love and appreciate their bodies regardless of social beauty standards, we foster a culture in which sexual expression is valued rather than condemned. This positive attitude can make women feel more at ease and confident about their sexual encounters, resulting in better and more rewarding relationships.

Accepting women's sexuality is a vital step in promoting female empowerment and body positivity. Understanding the diversity of women's sexual experiences, challenging cultural expectations, and fostering body positivity can help us build a world in which women feel free to express and investigate their sexuality without fear of criticism. Let us get together to celebrate and support all women's sexual experiences and desires.

Chapter 7

Embracing Authenticity And Growth

Accepting the fact that your life belongs to you is a genuinely fantastic experience. It means the end of concealing, self-sabotage, and excuses that keep you from being your true self and speaking your truth. Stop attaching to people and blaming them for your current situation. This freeing decision opens up a world of possibilities for you, taking you on a fantastic trip in which you hold the key to unlocking doors.

Recognize and value your self-worth. Surround yourself with genuine connections from your inner circle, people who treat you with compassion and respect. Your heart should not serve as a playground for others. It is critical to separate yourself from folks who cause unnecessary drama or sap your vitality with negativity.

Value your precious life by not spending it on those who refuse to grow or adapt. Respect yourself enough to leave settings that no longer benefit your well-being or impede your personal development. Having the courage to let go of things or people who no longer serve a constructive purpose exhibits self-awareness and trust in your intuition.

While it may take some time to acknowledge and accept these realizations, the trip is worthwhile. Trust the process and believe that what is meant for you will come to you. We all know when we're not in the right place, and it's critical to believe in ourselves and act appropriately to achieve clarity and inner peace.

Even if it is difficult to let go of individuals you care about, trust your instincts. Making decisive decisions is essential for personal development, and life may take us on unexpected paths. Over time, we learn to be resilient in the face of loss and develop feelings for things or people we never knew existed.

In a society full of external pressures and cultural expectations, being true, truly, and unashamedly yourself may be a transformative act of self-empowerment and personal development.

The Power of Authenticity

Authenticity is about accepting your genuine self, with all of its idiosyncrasies and shortcomings. It is about living in accordance with your own values, interests, and beliefs, rather than complying with external standards. When you allow yourself to be real, extraordinary things begin to happen.

Inner Peace
Authenticity relieves you of the pressure of pretending to be someone you are not. This newfound inner serenity enables you to direct your energies toward personal development.

Self-Discovery
Embracing authenticity promotes self-reflection and discovery. It assists you in identifying your particular strengths, interests, and life purpose.

Meaningful Connections
Authenticity encourages true interactions with others. When you are authentic, you attract others who value you for who you are, resulting in deeper, more lasting connections.

Empowerment
Authenticity is empowering. It empowers you to follow your goals, speak your truth, and conquer obstacles.

How to Embrace Authenticity

Self-Reflection
Take time to consider your values, beliefs, and passions. What makes you tick? What are your absolute must-haves in life?

Courageous vulnerability
Authenticity frequently entails being vulnerable. Share your ideas, emotions, and sensations with close friends or a support group.

Set boundaries
Establishing and communicating your boundaries is a critical component of authenticity. It exhibits self-respect and care.

Challenge the Comparison Trap
Resist the impulse to compare yourself to others. Remember that your experience is unique, and comparisons can undermine authenticity.

Cultivating Authenticity in Your Personal Development Journey

Define your goals
Set personal development goals that are consistent with your genuine self. What do you really want to achieve?

Track your progress
Maintain a journal to document your progress toward personal growth. Document your accomplishments, challenges, and learnings along the journey.

Celebrate your authenticity
Recognize and cherish the times when you have been completely authentic. Recognize the courage it requires.

Join the Community of Authenticity

Empowerment Groups:
Consider joining an empowerment circle or community of people who share your values and appreciate authenticity. Surrounding yourself with genuine individuals can be quite encouraging.

Personal Development Programs
These programs provide structured direction and resources for personal development in an authentic and supportive setting.

Adopting authenticity is a journey of self-discovery, empowerment, and personal growth rather than just a decision. It's about giving oneself permission to be completely yourself in a world that sometimes wants conformity. When you accept authenticity, you open the door to a life full of purpose, meaningful connections, and boundless possibilities.

So dare to be yourself. Accept your uniqueness. Celebrate your authenticity. Your personal growth journey begins when you acknowledge who you truly are and go on a road guided by your own beliefs and goals.

Trust in life, push aside fear and look for lessons in challenges. Allow yourself to go with the flow, enjoying each step on your personal path. May you have the strength to deeply honor yourself.

Conclusion

I remember when I was in high school, virginity meant everything. Being a virgin was not a universally positive trait, but it served as the axis around which the rest of your social life and reputation would revolve. There was scorn directed at girls on both sides of the divide, but it was critical that you assert your claim. If you were a virgin, you were meant to be a "prude" whose inability to get laid was very probably due to your habitually closed legs, or complete physical unattractiveness. It was humiliating to still be a virgin, especially when you were with a lover and so considered to be unwilling to "put out." It was your responsibility, after all.

Then, if you lost your virginity and it became public knowledge, you were tainted in some way. You had allowed some guy to get into your panties, and unless the sex was in the most ideal conditions with the boy you'd been dating nonstop for the previous two years, and surrounded by white rose petals, it was filthy. Apart from the numerous potential suitors who assumed you were careless about your sex once you were "opened for business," a lot of presumptions were made about you right away. If you strayed too far from the road of sexual tolerance, you'd be labeled a slut right away.

We were children, and kids are vicious. That is true. The labeling, categorizing, and prying aren't as open or intense as it was when you were all shut up in the same place five days a week, but it's still present. The underlying beliefs that fueled the heated social games surrounding sex at 16 remain in effect at 24, albeit more insidiously.

I recall how that made me despise other women. The point was, that the higher the premium on all of our individual sexuality at that age, the fiercer the rivalry for male favor. I let the viciously judgmental terms "slut," "whore," or "loose" stream from my mouth like poison, hoping it would settle on the females whose morals felt too far out of line for the tastes of teenage politics. She kissed my partner and slept with every guy in the group, all in the rear of her car parked in front of the school. These were all indiscretions that, for some

41

strange reason, upset us individually and harmed our collective reputation.

I still resist the need to evaluate another woman based on how she enjoys and expresses her sexuality. I still hesitate before discussing sex and my body, because we learned that it is not a woman's responsibility to divulge such things. They are skins to shed, cocoons from which we must emerge as much more evolved, compassionate humans. And we are actively attempting to eliminate the words that emphasize them. We understand what slut-shaming is and why it's horrible. This is a good thing and a move in the right way.

However, at some point, the words become little more than that. There are far more powerful ideas behind them, ideals that make a woman her own toughest critic. Even if we can teach one another not to call other girls filthy names or persuade her that there is no such thing as too much sex as long as it is healthy and consenting, how do we make her feel in control of her own body? Because the truth is that "slut" and the notions that surround it only exist in girls who are uneasy about themselves. When you hear the term whispered across a bar while another female parades past in a red dress and full confidence, the speaker isn't actually referring to this woman. It's herself. She was raised to believe that her worth is inextricably linked to that of that woman, and that wearing too tight a dress or having one too many drinks would diminish it.

Getting women to regard each other as free agents who can do whatever they want as long as they don't harm others and are free of moral judgments is one thing. But the first step is for women to regard their bodies as living and vital, deserving of all the happiness and pleasure they desire. We must learn that sexuality and joy are not limited resources that will be depleted if another woman takes too much. We can make our own, modify it, and provide enough for every individual we fall in love with, even if just for one night. Seeing ourselves as the primary driver of our own pleasure and directors of our own sexual development is the beginning and end of "slut," because the word means nothing if it is not employed as a value judgment. When every woman is satisfied with what sex means to her, the concept will be obsolete, but not before.

There is no way of not becoming a slut. There is only one way to embrace sex on your own terms, such that you are no longer outraged by someone else taking a different path. If I could talk to my 16-year-old self today, who was scared of sex and unsure of what was expected of her, I would urge her to forget about what boys desire. I would encourage her not to worry about what other females would think because everyone who talks is simply unhappy with themselves. I would advise her to focus on developing solid friendships, becoming closer to her family, and taking her time with anything she wants to pursue. Because the only remedy for "being a slut" is happiness, and only because it reminds us that such a foolish notion does not exist in the first place.

Made in the USA
Columbia, SC
25 August 2024

41142703R00024